Sales Framework

Implementation Guide

Sales Framework – Implementation Guide

Implementing a Profitable and Repeatable Sales Framework

Paul Freeman & David Bright

Disclaimer

The content provided herein is for educational purposes and does not take the place of professional legal or business advice consultation. Every effort has been made to ensure that the content provided in this guide is accurate and helpful for our readers at publishing time. However, this is not an exhaustive treatment of the subjects. No liability is assumed for losses or damages due to the information provided. You are responsible for your own choices, actions, and results. You should consult your attorney for your specific publishing and disclaimer questions and needs.

Copyright

Table of Contents

About This Document

Document Overview

The Implementing a Profitable and Repeatable Sales Framework leading practice is a guide to moving a sales opportunity from identification through proposal and delivery to the customer. This process is can also be called opportunity management. It provides descriptions of "best in class" business practices and detailed action plans for designing and implementing an effective sales framework and opportunity management system.

Intended Audience

This leading practice document is intended for the following audience:

- Executive Management
- Sales Management
- Delivery Management
- Project Management
- Sales Engineering

Why Is This Important?

The sales framework provided in this guide enables you to develop a structured approach to managing identified opportunities. Critical to your success is the ability to prioritize sales opportunities that have the best chance of success and managing those opportunities to closure. You must also be capable of effectively transferring the winning solution to your service delivery group for implementation. Finally, it is important you institute a process which allows for the analysis of both successful and unsuccessful sales opportunities and implementation of a continuous business improvement process.

What are the key performance indicators of a proper sales framework?

- Availability of sales-ready marketing content
- Initial account qualification tools
- Account planning in alignment with key partners
- Higher level design and quality assurance requirements
- Automated and repeatable sales process
- Increased win ratio to proposals generated

- Dollar revenue per opportunity in pipeline/closed

- Gross margin percentage per opportunity in pipeline/closed

- Velocity of opportunities – length of selling cycle

- Market expense per dollar revenue/gross margin

- Percent service revenue/gross margin in total revenue/gross margin

Managing by Metrics

The following foundation metrics are used to measure and manage repeatable sales framework and opportunity management improvements. More information on these metrics can be found in the Leading Practice document titled *Metrics Management Guide.*

Metric	Description
Revenue Mix Ratio	Revenue mix ratio identifies the number or percent of products, professional services, and maintenance contracts being sold by your company.
Attach Rate	Attach rate represents how many complementary products are sold for each primary product. For example, for every product that is sold, warranties, installation and other complementary products could be "attached" to the sale.
Win/Loss Ratio	Win / loss ratio is the number of sales won or lost represented by statistical numbers or economic value.
Mark Up	The amount or margin added above the burdened cost of a technical resource. This amount is considered Gross Profit when calculating the Cost of Good for professional services.
Blended Gross Margin	Blended Gross Margin is the gross margin attributed to the overall sales of products, services, and other offerings your company may provide.

Selling: Implementing a Profitable and Repeatable Sales Framework

A profitable and repeatable sales framework is the process by which you can manage and prioritize a pipeline of identified sales opportunities. Once your pre-sales process has worked through the discovery phase and identified an opportunity, it should be tracked through a standardized sales framework process that drives effectiveness through the sales and delivery lifecycle. The process acts as a Leading Practice to respond to an opportunity in a manner that gives your organization the best chance for success. It also provides a method of transferring the successful solution to your service delivery team for implementation. Finally, this leading practice incorporates a feedback system that analyzes wins and losses for the purpose of supporting a continual business improvement process.

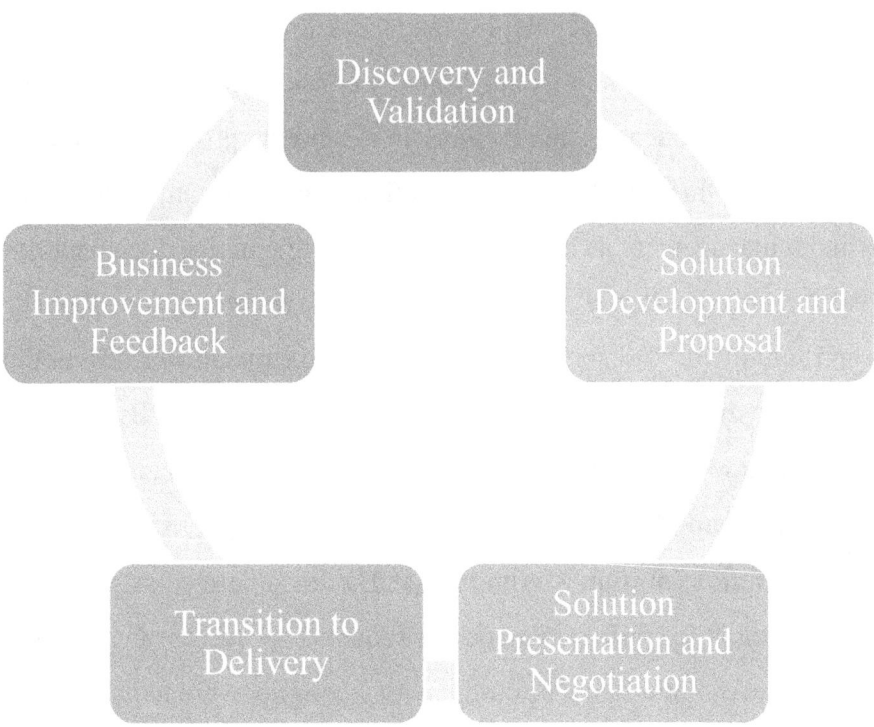

Within this leading practice the term "opportunity management" is used to refer to the method of proactively acting on and tracking a potential sale from identification through proposal development and eventually transitioning to your delivery team for implementation. Prior to identification, well defined sales and marketing processes need to be implemented that help you generate opportunities. These topics are discussed in detail within the series of "Selling" and "Marketing" leading practice documents. There are several key areas of interest that directly impact opportunity management and should be understood prior to implementing an opportunity management process as part of your sales framework include:

- **Business/Market/Relationship Development:** Once you have identified the accounts to pursue, you can begin your business development. Business development encompasses the marketing and sales development activities required to identify the business needs of, and opportunities to sell products or services to your targeted market. Business development precedes opportunity development and is critical to the generation of new opportunities.

- **Demand Generation:** Demand generation refers to stimulating the interest of prospective customers and developing leads in a territory, account, or other targeted customer areas. You would typically consider demand generation a marketing activity, but any team member in touch with prospects or customers could perform in this role. Demand generation is an important preamble to opportunity management as it relates to this leading practice document. Its activities create consistency in your selling process when they are aligned with sales and solution development activities. Demand generation leads turn into opportunities when they are properly qualified and developed. By aligning your demand generation activities with your overall opportunity management plan, you will create a stream of account leads that can turn into opportunities.

- **Sales Process and Solution Methodology:** Having a defined sales process and a skilled sales force are further components required for success in generating opportunities. An optimized sales force with a common vernacular and methodology for effective selling will be prepared to handle incoming opportunities effectively. Your field sales and pre-sales teams can employ effective questioning and solution-focused opportunity development skills to drive opportunities into this leading practice framework. Sales processes, tools and techniques for generating opportunities can be found in the series of "Selling" leading practices.

- **Opportunity Identification:** When you recognize that the customer's business will present many opportunities, you can identify them at any point during the sale or service delivery process. Developing an opportunity into a sale may include knowing where to log it and route it for pre-sales support within your organization. In most cases this is a prerequisite to the processes defined in this leading practice.

- **Collateral and Sales-Ready Content**: Being well prepared with sales collateral, case studies, customer testimonials, technical briefs, and other key information will increase the responsiveness and effectiveness of your sales team and support the generation of new opportunities.

- **Partner Program Usage**: Strategic and Manufacturer Partner offer a variety of sales, marketing, and leading practice materials to their resellers. Leveraging the Partner marketing and demand generation programs, in particular, can create a flow of incoming opportunities that will feed your opportunity management process. For more information on these programs, see your Partner field representatives for your specific programs.

- **Account Planning and Partner Alignment**: By building a strategic business relationship with Partners, you have the opportunity to collaborate with the Partner field team. Aligning your territory development, account planning, and go-to-market strategies will produce more cohesion with the Partner field account team. Using the Partner relationship effectively will help you qualify, develop, and close a higher percentage of your incoming opportunities.

Benefits of a Sales Framework

A well-developed sales framework and opportunity management process benefits your business by:

- Improving sales productivity by employing standardized processes for qualifying, tracking and responding to valid customer needs.

- Increasing your win ratio through the implementation of a strong opportunity assessment and validation process. This process determines the critical success factors needed to close new business based on the customer's needs and your company's strengths.

- Lowering cost of sales by focusing Account Management teams on opportunities that have a high percentage chance of closing.

- Identifying and mitigating risk associated with new opportunities.

- Increasing confidence in your sales forecasting through the use of standardized rules for defining the probability of closing sales opportunities.

- Facilitating successful implementations by creating a standardized turnover package and information sharing process.

- Providing for continual improvement through the employment of a Business Improvement Analysis and Feedback loop.

- Fostering strong communication between your sales teams and other functional areas within the organization.

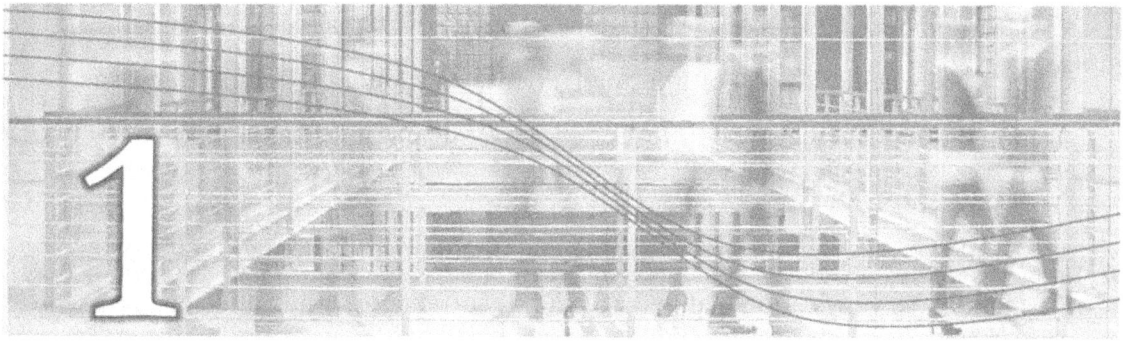

Chapter 1: Discovery and Validation

Upon identifying an opportunity, leading practice suggests your organization perform a comprehensive discovery and validation process. The purpose of this process is to take an in-depth look at the opportunity, determine its fit with your core capabilities, identify any inherent risks, and help decide whether you should commit resources to pursue an engagement. Should you decide to pursue the opportunity upon completion of the Discovery and Validation process; the critical success factors required to win the business will be identified. These critical success factors can then form the basis of the account strategy and subsequent solution development.

Opportunity Evaluation

Selling solutions involves identifying the customer's business needs as well as the technical platforms required to solve those business issues. The first step in the Discovery and Validation process is to determine if the solution required by the customer matches the core capabilities of your company. This initial step will help your team understand if the opportunity aligns with your company's business objectives for profitability, revenue mix and other factors and determine, at a high level, if you want to pursue it any further.

Customer Evaluation

Leading Practices suggest you perform an analysis of the customer to determine the viability of an opportunity, the risk factors associated with this client, and the positioning required by you to win the business. Areas of customer analysis you should perform include the following:

- Organization Review: In the organization review you should look at the client's organizational structure. Leading sales professionals fully understand who the decision makers are as well as the positive and negative influencers related to the opportunity

- Decision Making Process: All customers have an internal decision-making process, whether formal or informal. Your team should fully understand the process and surface any political or organizational issues that might positively or negatively affect your chances for success.

- Available Funding: Prior to pursuing an opportunity a Leading Practice would include the verification that the project has sufficient funding allocated and who within the client's organization controls that funding.

- Financial Stability: A top level review of the client's financial stability should be performed for projects of sufficient size to impact your own operations. Dunn & Bradstreet and/or annual reports for public companies are tools that can be used to determine your customer's financial stability.

- Potential Return on Investment (ROI): A return-on-investment analysis should be performed on any opportunity of substantial size (as determined by your executive team). The ROI must align with the financial objectives of your Company. In addition to ROI, a financial evaluation should identify key metrics such as expected net bookings and gross profit.

- Proposal costs: The proposal itself should be addressed as a standalone project including budgeted costs to develop. As a sales professional you should understand the "cost to win."

- Timeframes: Time frames should be estimated for both the proposal development and subsequent delivery with available resources identified.

Competitive Environment Analysis

In addition to fully understanding the client, Leading Practices suggest you analyze the competitive environment affecting any opportunity. Competitive Analysis serves to identify your strengths and those of your competitors as well as surface any gaps your proposal team will need to address. The following are included in Leading Practice Competitive analysis:

- **Number of competitors:** A straight forward count and initial ranking of competitors should be performed to understand not only the volume of firms vying for the business but also which firms can truly fulfill the customer's requirements.

- **Competitor's value-add/strengths:** Evaluate the strengths and weaknesses of your main competitors and utilize that data in the development of your proposal. Strengths/weaknesses could represent financial, technological, geographic, skills, pricing, or other key attributes.

- **Relationship to client:** Many times, a competitor is uniquely positioned with the client through strong contacts or relationships within the organization. You should identify and understand these relationships for the purpose of crafting proposals that differentiate your company.

Collaborative Partnering

Many times, a total solution will dictate you align with a third party Independent Software Vendor (ISVs) or other firm with key products or services that can complement your core offerings. It takes time and good communication to involve third parties in an opportunity. Early teaming and subcontracting decisions allow your company to select the best partners, develop a mutual plan for pursuit of the opportunity and to obtain good pricing. How well you define the relationship including scope, roles, and responsibilities, as well as determining pricing, will affect how successful the sales effort will be.

- Identify gaps in your ability to deliver the opportunity and determine required teaming partners (ISV).

- Ensure that the teaming partner(s) align with your core capabilities.

- Assess the teaming Partner's ability to deliver per the Scope of Work.

- Leading Partners should always determine the financial stability and reputation of third parties.

Critical Success Factors

Critical Success Factors are the four or five key attributes you must incorporate into the solution and proposal to be responsive to the client's business issues and best position your company to secure the opportunity. The success factors are derived from the Discovery and Validation process and provide your team with a solid roadmap to a successful engagement.

Go/No Go Decision

Upon completion of the Discovery and Validation process and determination of the critical success factors required to win the business, you are now positioned to make a Go/No Go decision. A "Go" decision means the opportunity aligns well with your company's business goals and core competencies, has strong benefit/cost ratio (potential profits versus cost of proposal), and that you are well positioned to win.

A "No Go" decision simply means that you are better off allocating resources to other opportunities that align better across the same range of opportunity attributes.

Example of Go/No Go indicators include:

Go Indicators	No Go Indicators
Sole sourced opportunity	Highly competed opportunity
The opportunity is strategic to your business	The opportunity is a commodity-based solution
The customer is looking for the best value-based solution	The opportunity is competed on low price
You have strong relationships and past performance history with the client	You are blindly responding to a Request for Proposal (RFP)
You have relationships with third party teaming partners which allow for the delivery of a value-based proposal	Your ability to respond technically is sound but will most likely land as a higher priced solution
You have an opportunity to attach high margin products or services in order to meet revenue mix and profitability goals.	Customer is only interested in getting products at the lowest price and is not interested in any services or value-added offerings.

Action Plan

Step 1:   Conduct an Opportunity Evaluation that identifies your customer's business need and determine if the solution required aligns with the core capabilities of your company.

Step 2:   Administer a Customer Evaluation to determine the opportunities viability, risk factors, and required positioning.

Step 3:   Perform a Competitive Environment Analysis to identify strengths and weaknesses and frame out the competitive landscape.

Step 4:   Identify any teaming required to round out the best total solution for your client's business need.

Step 5:   Develop the four or five Critical Success Factors that must be incorporated into your solution.

Step 6:   Make a Go/No Go decision based on the outcomes of the Discovery and Opportunity Validation process.

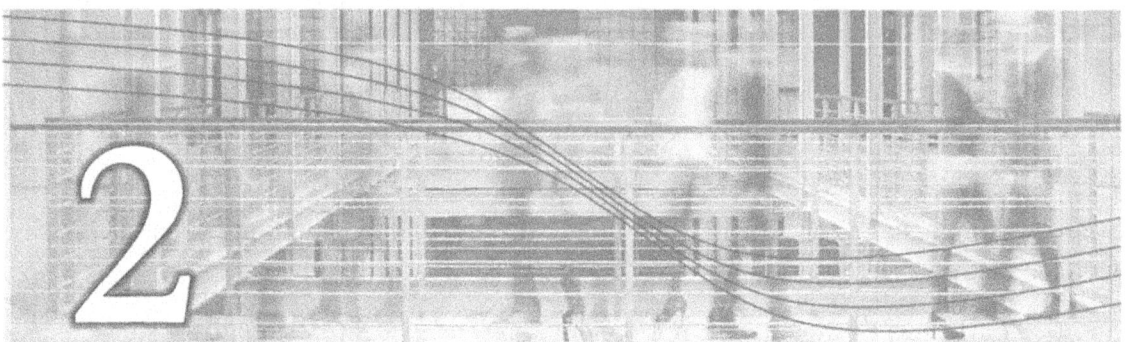

Chapter 2. Solution Development and Proposal Strategy

Upon completion of the Opportunity Discovery and Validation phase, it is time to roll the information garnered into a viable solution for your client. The solution development process combines the critical success factors with technical solution design and pricing to create a proposal strategy. The leading practice proposal strategy seeks to deliver a high value proposition to meet your client's business needs.

Customer Requirements

Managing the opportunity through the solution development phase typically requires your team to gain a greater understanding of the client's needs. Sales professionals typically develop an internal team with technical and business acumen to identify and document all the customer's requirements. Asking intelligent questions and demonstrating a firm understanding of the needs of the business also build your credibility with the client. Often it is advantageous, if not required, to engage the Sales Engineering team to gain a greater understanding of the technical options affecting the solution.

- **Solution Scoping Business Requirements:** This part of the discussion should focus on the strategic and tactical needs of the business itself, without regard to any product or service specific recommendations. Your customer's underlying business issues will need to be completely recognized to drive the technical solution.

- **Technical Scoping Technical Requirement:** This phase of the discussion should focus on the current IT operating environment, benchmark what is in place today and identify solutions for the future. Leading practice questions focus on infrastructure, systems, networks, and other operating platforms.

Developing a Design Solution

The design should be developed to address your client's business issues. A thorough design must also be cognizant of your client's budget, future migration to new technologies, and on-going maintenance and support needs.

Creating a Unique Value Proposition

The Value Proposition is a clear and succinct statement (e.g., 2-4 sentences) that is the foundation of "what's in it" for your customer. The critical success factors defined in the discovery phase should form the basis of both your technical solution as well as the value proposition. Leading practice value propositions should explain to the potential Client and stakeholders the solutions unique, value-creating features. The most effective value proposition contains a specific benefit, which is the financial value of using your solution. A well-conceived value proposition should distinguish your firm from other competitors. It should clearly communicate the solution in a manner that allows your team to sell based on value versus price.

Preparing a Scope of Work (SOW)

The scope of work should take into consideration all aspects of your solutions design and deployment. A leading practice SOW provides the customer with a clearly articulated description of the system components and functionality. It should also explain how your solution fulfills the business issues identified in the discovery phase through a clearly crafted value proposition.

A well-crafted SOW may include:

- Engineering criteria and solution fulfillment
- Installation methodology
- Timing and high-level project milestones
- Integration mapping
- Service and support expectations and solutions
- Migration path and roadmap to future growth

Developing a Cost Model and Pricing Options

Critical to the development of the customer facing price is the creation of a cost estimate. The cost estimate forms the foundation of the solution budget and will be used to develop your total price. A leading practice will utilize the cost estimating process to develop a detailed understanding of all costs and identify subsequent financial risks and rewards.

The pricing exercise seeks to strike a balance between the value of the solution to the customer and the value to your company. Market forces, risk factors, timing, and target margins should all be analyzed when developing the final price.

The inherent "costs" associated with the delivery of your solutions are also a key consideration in the development of pricing standards. Engineering costs, both pre-sale and post-sale, must be factored into your "markup strategy" for those resources. Engineering resources too heavily discounted may result in a non-optimum business situation.

Additionally, the concept of sales mix must be taken into account. When you have an opportunity to bundle high-price professional services with product and warranty services, you can create a blended margin well above what you might make for product only sales.

By ensuring that professional services are properly priced and that solutions have both product services and attached warranty, you will increase the overall size of the deal and gain the full margin potential.

Action Plan

Step 1: Review the critical success factors developed in the discovery and validation phase.

Step 2: Schedule follow up meeting(s) with your potential client to evaluate and fully understand both the technical and underlying business needs.

Step 3: Design a solution that takes into consideration your client's budget, future migration to new technologies, and on-going maintenance and support needs.

Step 4: Create a unique value proposition that clearly communicates the solution in a manner that allows your team to sell based on value versus price.

Step 5: Prepare a scope of work that takes into consideration all aspects of the solutions design and deployment.

Step 6:   Develop a comprehensive cost model based on the solution design and competitive pricing options. Review current markup and blended sales mix to ensure proper pricing.

Step 7:   Perform a detailed cost and pricing review with appropriate stakeholders.

Chapter 3. Solution Presentation and Negotiation

Preparing a responsive, persuasive, and definitive solutions proposal is essential to winning new business. The process starts with the development of a proposal strategy and ends with a final written document that is reviewed and signed by the appropriate decision makers within the customer's organization. Your proposal should be developed by a team represented by sales, technical, logistics, service support, finance, and legal. The team that presents and negotiates the proposal with your potential customer is part of this larger team. The presentation team must have complete and thorough knowledge of the customer's business and solution needs, along with knowledge of the proposed solution and value proposition.

The Presenter

The presentation is traditionally delivered by the sales person who manages the account. The presenter is responsible for organizing all aspects of the meeting including logistics, attendees, and presentation format. For large solution projects, include your technical support engineer and senior management when possible. The presentation team must have in-depth knowledge of the customer's business and solution needs. The team needs to be able to address all your customer's concerns.

The Proposal (Statement of Work)

The written proposal is the foundation of the final presentation. A properly designed and written proposal will address all aspects of a customer's requirements with a detailed description of your specific products and services. The proposal should communicate the customer's needs and the capability of your solution to satisfy those needs.

The proposal process coincides with project planning, costing, and pricing. The basic components of a proposal are to:

- Describe your capabilities and products

- Explain how your solution resolves key issues

- Outline your value proposition

- Explain your Pricing Structure

- Outline your delivery and implementation plan

The proposal may become part of a contract between the customer and your company. It is a legal document that may include elements such as penalties for non-delivery or tardiness.

The Presentation

A well-designed presentation will convey your technical solution to the customer. You should highlight the value proposition to assist in differentiating yourself from the competition. You should develop an extensive library of technical presentations that can be integrated into your final solution.

The Negotiation

Negotiations can occur throughout the proposal preparation, or after the presentation. Formal negotiations are generally triggered by an informal notice from the customer of an award, pending acceptable contract terms.

The challenge is to negotiate a contract that protects your legal, business, and financial interests while delivering a satisfactory solution to the customer. Start by identifying the upper and lower boundaries of acceptable pricing, delivery time frame, and implementation conditions. Pre-identify conditions that would require your team to stop negotiations and disengage with the customer. It is important that the negotiation process allow flexibility to address last minute changes.

Action Plan

Step 1: Designate a lead presenter and negotiator.

Step 2: Develop the Presentation.

- Prepare a presentation supporting the proposal or statement of work (SOW).

- Review all aspects of the presentation with appropriate experts including service support, technical experts, logistics, finance, and legal.

- Review the presentation incrementally; at inception, first draft and final draft.

- Describe your capability to support the proposal.

Step 3: Prepare for Meeting.

- Set date, time, and location of presentation.
- Verify key decision makers will be present.
- Verify presentation props and equipment are working

Step 4: Deliver the Presentation.

- Present the solution
- Highlight the value proposition
- Set customer expectations

Step 5: Negotiations.

- For a written record of the transaction, document negotiations as they progress.
- Involve selected project managers in the contract negotiation process.
- Sign the final proposal, SOW, or contract.

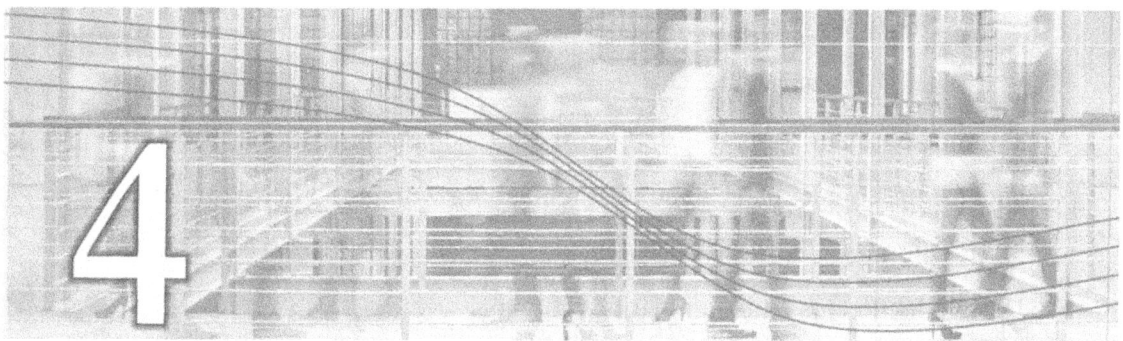

Chapter 4. Transition to Delivery Team

After successfully closing an opportunity with the client a leading practice will transfer the knowledge and criteria that went into developing the solution to the delivery team. Typically, this process includes the proposal team and your Project Manager. The benefit of having a defined process for this step is to eliminate any confusion in the hand-off process that could result in implementation delays or customer confusion. Many eager sales representatives have moved a closed deal to delivery without proper contracts, purchase orders, or credit applications in place. These types of operational misalignments can cause friction not only between your sales and delivery staff members, but also with your customers who may be anxious to get the project started.

Bid Book

Professional sales proposal teams develop a bid book that contains all the pertinent information the Project Manager will need to successfully implement the solution with the client. In lieu of a fully developed bid book, the proposal team must, at a minimum, transfer this knowledge to the Project Manager verbally. Bid books should contain the following information.

- Business Requirements Definition
  - Statement of the client's business issue (description of what need your solution is solving)
- Pricing approach and options that the customer may have accepted
- Signed contract documents
- Any unique customer requirement or expectations
  - Project Description
  - Written scope of work

- o Technology requirements
- o Bill of materials
- Teaming partners—this information should include third party SOW, contract documents, contact names and numbers, along with any other pertinent information
- Design documents and engineering drawings
- Service Level Agreements and any maintenance or warranty information
- Client contact information
- Delivery Requirements
- Major project milestones and time frame commitments
- Identified project constraints or challenges
- Resource mapping and cost basis
- Deliverables and project close out process
- Financial goals and targets

Communication plan to include sales, sales support, project team members, and your client organization

Project Handoff Meeting

Ideally a project handoff meeting will be held to formally transfer the information and bid book from your proposal team to the project manager. In these meetings all stakeholders including sales, sales engineers, systems engineers, estimators, and technical writers should be present to ensure that all facets of the solution and proposal knowledge are completely understood by the Project Manager. At the conclusion of the meeting, the Project Manager should be fully equipped with the knowledge and back up materials required to deliver a successful project. At this point your delivery team should take possession of the opportunity.

Action Plan

Step 1:   Develop bid book that should include the following:

- Business requirements definition

- Project description

- Delivery requirements

Step 2: Schedule and hold a project handoff meeting.

- Include all stakeholders

- Transfer knowledge and ownership to your service delivery team

Step 3: Ensure that a customer communication plan is place during the transition process.

Chapter 5. Business Improvement Analysis and Feedback

As part of a comprehensive Sales framework and opportunity management process it is important to close the loop on each opportunity to determine areas of process strength as well as identify stages that need improvement. This process can be implemented with regularly scheduled meetings that include all the key stakeholders in the opportunity management process.

Evaluate

Quantify what is or is not working in your opportunity management life cycle. Include information gained from your data tracking and statistics process, stakeholder feedback, and customer input. Standard questions can be developed that tie to the objectives set for the opportunity management process. Sample questions might include:

- Has the **win/loss rate** increased or decreased?

- Are the **revenue forecasts** more accurate?

- Has Gross Margin improved?

- Has customer satisfaction increased?

- Is the firm gaining repeat or annuity-based business?

- Has **attach rate** or **blended sales mix** increased?

Refine

The opportunity management process is not static. Customer needs change—internal personnel and processes migrate while the company's culture evolves. You should look for trends that affect the process and constantly fine tune the stages. By performing regularly scheduled reviews, the sales framework and opportunity management process will remain active and a vital component of your success.

Ongoing Support

Many times, a newly implemented process is met with uncertainty and viewed as additional work by the various stakeholders. Employees will watch management closely for signs of commitment. It is important for your management team to constantly reinforce the importance of the sales framework and opportunity management process.

Action Plan

Step 1:   Schedule periodic process review meetings

- Evaluate the process by listening to stakeholder feedback
- Refine the process for continual improvement
- Provide ongoing support

Chapter 6. Tracking and Statistics

Daily and weekly activity reports that demonstrate how effectively you manage an opportunity once it has been identified are the cornerstone for managing the processes outlined in this guide. A regimented approach to statistics and statistical analysis that focuses on the collection and evaluation of core data will improve your results significantly.

Key metrics can be tracked in a specialized software application or in an internally developed spreadsheet. Sales and management teams should monitor key statistics on a weekly and monthly basis to better understand the volume of opportunities that flow through the business.

Effective tracking and statistics will help you with:

- Forecasting revenue with improved accuracy
- Capacity planning across all facets of your sales, estimating, and service delivery functions
- Cash flow forecasting
- Win/loss percentages and intelligence
- Visibility into deal structure, including types of projects, customer information, average deal constructs, and naturally occurring vertical market expertise

Tracking key statistics will provide you with advanced notice regarding issues that arise with customers or with ineffective sales activities. In addition, areas for improvement and growth will become apparent.

- The number of statistics tracked will depend on these factors:

- The granularity of the details you want to manage.

- How sophisticated the automated tracking tools are.

At a minimum, you should track one or two key statistics for each stage in the opportunity management process. Examples of statistics tracked for a given period are:

- Prospecting

- Opportunities identified

- Decision maker identified

- Discovery and Validation

- Opportunities qualified.

- Customer need identified

- Customer discovery and validation meetings held

- Go/No go decisions made

- Proposal Development

- Proposals generated or declined

- Up-sell opportunities generated

- Presentation

- Sales won, lost, or abandoned

- Add-on business generated

- ID-to-win percentages

Capturing this data will also allow you to create standard metrics that can be compared to industry and internal benchmarks. These might include:

- Leads by date, customer, or other segment

- Lead-to-opportunity conversion

- Lead-to-win conversion

Using the statistical data collected will help you increase overall effectiveness of the sales framework and opportunity management process. By reviewing the data and identifying trends, you will be better prepared to address business issues before they reach a critical point.

Examples include:

If wins are declining, your team can evaluate why losses are occurring and make adjustments to pricing, solution development process, or some other factor contributing to the loss.

Conversely, if statistics show progress, you can reinforce those behaviors and integrate the winning activities into core processes.

By using statistics, you can eliminate much of the guesswork involved in the selling process and foster an environment where constant refinement and improvement are the norm. By having this information readily available, you can develop strategies, execute plans, and measure results on an ongoing basis.

Action Plan

Step 1:   Set objectives for tracking and statistics.

- Improved closure rates
- Accurate forecasting
- Cost reduction
- Improved communications
- Enhanced management visibility

Step 2:   Define stages of your sales framework and opportunity management cycle.

- Prospect
- Discovery and validation
- Proposal development
- Presentation
- Closed sales
- Transfer knowledge and ownership to your service delivery team

Step 3:   Identify critical handoffs between functional teams.

Step 4:   Develop statistics and elements to be tracked.

- Customer information
- Revenue potential
- Capture rate
- Gross Profit
- Step 5: Implement tracking tools.
- Assess tools
- Assign responsibilities
- Define roles
- Create/purchase tools

Chapter 7. How Do You Measure Success?

An effective sales framework and opportunity management process will drive success across your business in several ways. A well-conceived and implemented framework should enable you to prioritize opportunities and craft solutions that give you the best chance for success. This framework will increase the number of deals you win as a percentage of the total number of opportunities you identify and actively pursue.

Through the discovery and validation process, each opportunity will be evaluated against the financial criteria set forth in your business plan. Only opportunities that meet the desired criteria for gross revenue and profit will be sought after.

An effective sales framework will increase your total revenue, gross profit margin, or both. In addition, by implementing a solid sales framework and opportunity management process your proposal teams will only pursue opportunities that you have a solid chance of winning. By focusing on these types of opportunities and disregarding others that stand to waste your team's time, the cost of developing each proposal will decrease.

Finally, the sales framework and opportunity management process helps you truly understand the underlying business needs of your client and develop solutions that fulfill those needs. The process also creates a dependable and repeatable process for transitioning the proposed solution to your delivery team to implement. By developing creative solutions and implementing them seamlessly, your customer satisfaction will increase.

www.ingramcontent.com/pod-product-compliance
Lightning Source LLC
Chambersburg PA
CBHW081024170526
45158CB00010B/3149